COWLEY PUBLICATIONS is a ministry of the brothers of the Society of Saint John the Evangelist, a monastic order in the Episcopal Church. Our mission is to provide books and resources for those seeking spiritual and theological formation. COWLEY PUBLICATIONS is committed to developing a new generation of writers and teachers who will encourage people to think and pray in new ways about spirituality, reconciliation, and the future.

INCARNATION

INCARNATION

New and Selected Poems for Spiritual Reflection

Irene Zimmerman

A COWLEY PUBLICATIONS BOOK

Lanham, Chicago, New York, Toronto, and Plymouth, UK

Published in the United States of America by Cowley Publications, a division of the Society of Saint John the Evangelist.
No portion of this book may be reproduced, stored in or introduced into a retrieval system, or transmitted, in any form or by any means—including photocopying—without the prior written permission of Cowley Publications, except in the case of brief quotations embedded in critical articles and reviews.

Library of Congress Cataloging-in-Publication Data

Zimmerman, Irene.
   Incarnation : new and selected poems for spiritual reflection / Irene Zimmerman.
       p. cm.
    ISBN 1-56101-256-4 (pbk. : alk. paper)
    1. Christian poetry, American. 2.   Spiritual life—Poetry.
I. Title.
    PS3576.I5115I53 2004
    811'.54—dc22

                                                         2004006692

Cover design: Jennifer Hopcroft

This book was printed in the United States of America on acid-free paper.

A Cowley Publications Book
Published by Rowman & Littlefield Publishers, Inc.
A wholly owned subsidiary of
The Rowman & Littlefield Publishing Group, Inc.
4501 Forbes Boulevard, Suite 200, Lanham, Maryland 20706
http://www.rowmanlittlefield.com

10 Thornbury Road, Plymouth PL6 7PP, United Kingdom

Distributed by National Book Network

PROLOGUE: "IN THE BEGINNING WAS THE WORD"
Incarnation   12

I FIRST COVENANT WORDS

Creation of Eve   14
First Forgiveness   15
First Parenting   17
Sarah's Laughter   18
Exodus   19
Ruth Gleaning   21
What if Hannah Hadn't   22
Jonah: A Fable   23

II "AND THE WORD BECAME FLESH"

Dialogue   26
"How Can This Be, Since I Am a Virgin?"   27
Women Weaving   28
Mary Song   29
Song of Zechariah   30
Unto His Own   31
Christmas Sky   32
The Creatures' Christmas   33
Theophany   34
Jew-EL   35
First Word   36
Litany for Ordinary Time   37
Growing Pains   38
Mary Pondered All These Things   39

III "You Are My Beloved Son"

John the Baptist: The Passover   42
Beloved Son   43
The Testing (A Triptych)   44
1. Loaves of Stone
2. The Reign of God
3. From the Pinnacle

IV "Behold, I Come to Do Your Will"

Cana Wine   50
Healing of the Paralytic   53
Storm at Sea   55
Gerasene Demoniac   57
Homecoming   59
Ecstasy's End   60
Like a Little Child: A Story in Two Voices   61
Blind Trust   62
Firstborn Sons and the Widow of Nain   63
"She Has Shown Great Love"   64
Faith Power   66
When a Little Was Enough   67
Bethany Decisions   69
Woman Un-Bent   70
Jesus Preaches from the Boat   71
The Lost Parable   72
Father and Son: Two Prodigals   74
Jesus and Zacchaeus: A Short Story   76
Encounter with the Canaanite Woman   77
Expanding the Mission   79
Discipleship   80
At Jacob's Well (A Triptych)   81
1. Exchange
2. Reconciliation

3. To Jesus at the Well
Woman Taken in Adultery   84
Return of Lazarus   86
Anointings in Bethany   87

V "INTO YOUR HANDS I COMMEND MY SPIRIT"

Entry into Jerusalem   90
Overturning Tables: Reclaiming the Temple   91
Legacy   92
Last Lesson   94
And It Was Night   96
Mount of Olives   97
Agony   98
Betrayal   99
Stabat Mater   100
Jesus Comforts the Women   101
The Nailing   102
The Game   103
Crucifixion   104
Many Women Were Also There   105
Pietà   106

VI "HE IS RISEN. . . . GO TELL THE OTHERS"

Paschal Paradox   108
Liturgy   109
Easter Song   110
Resurrection   111
Easter Witnesses   112
The Women of Mark 16:8   114
Emmaus Journey   115
Primacy   116
Healing Touch   117
The Accused   118

Pontius Pilate at the Therapist   119
Toward Reconciliation   120
Rock Restored   121
Pentecost: Harvest Feast   123

VII MULLING THE WORD

Homemaker God   126
A Woman's Journey in Discipleship   127
Holy Ground   129
Learning to Trust   130
Yahweh, My Heritage, My Cup   131
Apple Picking: Eden Revisited   132
In This Fog   133
Emmanuel: God with Us   134
A Different Kind of King   135
Feast of St. Paul   136
On the Way to Easter   137
God of Shelter, God of Shade   139
Companion   140
Life-Giving   141
A Celibate Dialogues with God   142
Paschal Mystery   143
Prayer for a Happy Death   144
Wait for Me, Jesus   145
As It Was in the Beginning   146
As Jesus Dies   147
"Unless the Grain of Wheat Falls"   148
In His Mother's Arms   150
Our Father Our Mother   151
Commissioning   152

EPILOGUE: "I AM WITH YOU ALWAYS,
   TO THE END OF THE AGE"
   I Am with You Always   154

PROLOGUE

"IN THE BEGINNING WAS THE WORD"

INCARNATION

In careful hands
God held the molten world—
fragile filigree
of unfinished blown glass.

Then Mary's word: *Yes!*
rose like a pillar of fire,
and Breath blew creation
into Christed crystal.

I
FIRST COVENANT WORDS

CREATION OF EVE

(GENESIS 2:20–23)

(inspired by a wood sculpture of Herman Falke, SCJ)

God plunges headfirst
down the Eden sky
to midwife Eve from Adam-mud.

See how she steps from the clay
of Adam's sleeping side,
grows, blossoms, lithe and slim.

Oh, what a God-good,
gracious surprise awaits him
when Adam opens his eyes

and beholds the exquisite flower
that bloomed from his flesh
while he slept!

She is almost finished.
God's hand hovers, lingers
at the heaven of her freshly formed fingers.

FIRST FORGIVENESS

The usually mild evening breeze
became a wailing wind
when the gates clanged shut behind them.

They shivered despite their leathery clothes
as they searched for the fragrant blossoms
they'd grown accustomed to sleep on,
but found only serpentine coils
that bit and drew blood from their hands.

It was Eve who discovered the cave.
When she emerged, she saw Adam
standing uncertainly at the entrance.

A river of fire flooded her face
as she remembered his blaming words—
"The woman you gave me,
she gave me fruit from the tree,
and I ate."

"Spend the night wherever you choose,"
she told him bitterly.
"You needn't stay with me."

Long afterwards, when even the moon's
cold light had left the entrance
and she'd made up a word
for the hot rain running from her eyes,
she sensed Adam near her in the dark.

His breath shivered on her face.
"Eve," he moaned,
"I'm sorry. Forgive me."

In the darkness between them
the unfamiliar words
waited, quivering.
She understood their meaning
when she touched his tears.

FIRST PARENTING

In early years, while Adam tilled the fields
and Eve filled her lap with baby boys and girls,
they watched attentively for signs of aberration,
pounced hard on spats between the two- and three-
year-olds, planted frequent kisses on each child's
cheek, and tried to model love between them.

Later, as their growing sons and daughters
left the house, arm in arm, to play their made-up games,
they followed them with anxious admonitions—
"Don't fight! Take care of one another!"—knowing
they had brought a blight into their children's souls.

In later years of grieving for their twin sons—
the one whose blood had reddened the yellow grain
of sacrifice, the other branded for all time
as murderer—they asked each other,
"What could God have been thinking of
to give us power to choose to love or hate?"

Gradually, as Adam's handsome curls turned white
and Eve's beloved face shriveled like an apple,
they saw that God had led them back, if not
to Paradise itself, to love at least—
the best of what that early world had offered.

"Will our children live in peace after we're gone?"
they wondered in the end as they came to know
the pain of powerlessness and something of
an unfathomable God who dared to take
the risk of losing them, for their own freedom's sake.

SARAH'S LAUGHTER
(GENESIS 18:1–15)

When Abraham had hurried back
to the three Strangers with bread
and meat, milk and curds,
Sarah, obediently hiding her faded
beauty behind the tent flaps,
watched them feasting beneath the oak.

From there the Strangers' words
came winging to where she stood—
in shocked disbelief at first,
having grown old and used to
the sterile disfavor of Abraham's God,
then exploding in peals of laughter
that ricocheted off the oaks of Mamre
and the stony hills of promise.

"How many can you count, Sarah?"
Abraham asked as they held each other
beneath a blanket of stars.
"How many children will there be?"

The words set her off again,
and Abraham too,
with irrepressible mirth
till the hills whooped and hollered
and the stars blazed their *Aha*
in the pregnant desert night.

EXODUS

(EXODUS 14 & 15)

What a night it is—Israel caught between
Egypt and the sea! The sea whistling, howling;
wild-eyed sheep and cattle stampeding;
women and children screaming;
clouds rolling up in great white wheels,
rolling over the plains and the Egyptians;
lightning shattering the rocky beach;
thunder roaring like the very breath of God!

Moses stands on the edge of the world.
What will he say to the men filled with rage
for consenting to this hopeless flight?
to the women watching with mute, accusing eyes?

He feels the power of the staff in his hand.
The Lord himself will fight for you!

The Lord, they scoff. *How? With what?*
Will you scare the sea with your stupid stick?

The staff pulses in his hand.
You have only to keep still! he shouts in the wind.

What a night it is—wind howling, splitting the sea;
six hundred thousand men with their women and children
rushing pell-mell between towering cliffs of water;
Pharaoh closing in with his soldiers and chariots.

Moses' arm drops with the weight of the staff.
What a night it is—watery cliffs thundering down;
Egyptians, horses, wind shrieking;
chariots crashing, floundering, sinking;
waves booming up the beach, spitting up the debris
of broken Egypt at the feet of dancing Israel.
Miriam leads the chant: *Let us sing praise*
to the Holy One who saved us
this night—this very night.

RUTH GLEANING

(RUTH)

(inspired by a wood sculpture of Herman Falke, SCJ)

Her feet firmly planted
to support her daring reach
across the butternut wood,
Ruth the Moabite
leans far out
with pendulous breasts
and braided hair

to where Boaz stands
pondering the gleaned grain
with hands clasped behind him,
eyes closed—a tiny man,
a mere knot, unaware
of his imminent
harvesting.

Before the night is done
Ruth will graft herself onto
the Israel-tree
to glean a son
for Elimelech,
for Naomi,
for the Bread to be.

What if Hannah Hadn't?
(I Samuel)

What if Hannah hadn't prayed for a son
and wouldn't have had one?

If Samuel, then,
would not have been,

he wouldn't have left his mother's knee
at age three, obviously,

and moved to the temple for room and board
with ancient Eli and the Lord,

and Eli would have slept all night,
undisturbed by the threefold sound and sight

of persistent young Sam
and his "Here I am."

If Hannah hadn't prayed for a son,
would she have had one?

How much does God depend
on the prayers we send?

Jonah: A Fable
(Jonah)

God asked Jonah to save Nineveh,
but the stubborn fellow refused to obey
and instead set sail in the opposite way.

When a violent storm almost did them in,
the sailors drew lots, discovered his sin,
and dumped him overboard to save their skin.

As Jonah floundered in the sea's rock and roll,
soon to be one for whom the bells toll,
along swam a creature that swallowed him whole.

For three days he rode in the belly of the whale.
It traveled full speed without need of a sail
and safely delivered him, hearty and hale,

to the fore-ordained shore of his destination
where at last Jonah preached to the Ninevite nation,
pointing the way to eternal salvation.

Moral:
*If you stubbornly get yourself lost at sea,
don't complain about God's whale of delivery.*

II

"And the Word
Became Flesh"

DIALOGUE
(LUKE 1:5–20)

Zechariah stood at the altar and said,
"I don't believe it, Lord. It cannot be!
For twenty years we prayed for a son,
Elizabeth and I. I cannot see
our words should now first reach you, when
we're both too old to rear a child.
It's not so easy nowadays
to keep a son from running wild
and teach him to honor your ways.
You come too late, Lord. It cannot be."

"Zechariah," said the Lord, "my foolish man!
So long I've been with you, and can
you still doubt me—you, my high priest?
Have no fears about your power
to rear this child. When his hour
comes, he *must* run wild.
You'll later learn to understand his part.
But now, my people hear your word
and think you speak *my* will.
I cannot let you prattle
out of such an untaught heart.
Peace, dear foolish man. Be still."

"How Can This Be,
Since I Am a Virgin?"
(Luke 1:34)

Your world hung in the balance of her *yes* or *no*.
Yet, "She must feel absolutely free," You said,
and chose with gentle sensitivity not to go
Yourself—to send a messenger instead.

I like to think You listened in at that interview
with smiling admiration and surprise
to that humble child who—
though she didn't amount to much in Jewish eyes,
being merely virgin, not yet come to bloom—
in the presence of that other-worldly Power
crowding down the walls and ceiling of her room,
did not faint or cry or cower
and could not be coerced to enflesh Your covenant,
but asked her valid question first
before she gave her full and free consent.

I like to think You stood
to long applaud such womanhood.

WOMEN WEAVING
(LUKE 1:39–55)

Afterwards, Mary moved from fear
(*Will they drag me to the stoning place?*)
to pain (*Will Joseph doubt my faithfulness?*)
to trust (*I fear no evil—Thou art with me.*)
and back again to fear. "I must go to my cousin,"
she said, and set out in haste for Judea.

As her feet unraveled the warp and woof
of valleys and hills, darkness and days
from Nazareth to Elizabeth,
Mary wove the heart of her Son.

When her newly-womaned cousin came,
Elizabeth, wise old weaver herself
for several months by then, instantly
saw the signs and heavily ran to meet her.

"Who am I," she called, "that the mother
of my Lord should come to visit me?"
and helplessly held her sides as laughter
shuttled back and forth inside her.

Then Mary sang the seamless song
she'd woven on the way.

MARY SONG
(LUKE 1:39–55)

I ran the road from Nazareth
to share my news, Elizabeth:

I could not bear alone the flame
(my spirit sings God's sacred name!)

that sears my soul and sets God's will
ablaze throughout the House of Israel.

The Holy One has come to bless
and fill my waiting emptiness!

Elizabeth, come sing with me.
Your cousin dances with divinity!

Song of Zechariah
(Luke 1:59–79)

At the circumcision of his son,
relatives and neighbors came
to speak for Zechariah of the tied
tongue. The child, they concurred,
would bear his worthy father's name.
But during her husband's silence,
old Elizabeth had found her voice.
"His name will be John," she said.

Why this strange, unprecedented choice,
the relatives and neighbors wondered.
Armed with writing instrument,
back they went to poor, dumb Zechariah.
But during the long confinement,
as young Mary and Elizabeth
spoke about the missions of their sons,
he had listened and grown wise.

Straightaway, he wrote: "His name is John."
He caught Elizabeth's smiling eyes,
felt his old tongue loosen, found his voice,
    sang of God's tender mercy,
    sang of the breaking dawn,
    sang of the prophet, their son,
    who would make straight the way
    for the long awaited One.

UNTO HIS OWN
(LUKE 2:7–16)

Homeless that first night—
one more statistic
to add to the census,
one more mouth to feed.

Only the shepherds,
having nothing to lose
except a little sleep,
came to see.

CHRISTMAS SKY
(MATTHEW 2:9)

That once-in-a-world-time night
even the stars, otherwise
so distant in their ancient skies,
came to adore the in-the-beginning Light.

THE CREATURES' CHRISTMAS
(LUKE 2:7)

"Do not be afraid," the angel said,
so the creatures crowded around his bed.

Incense smoked from the patient ox
as it breathed on the child in its old feedbox.

The donkey, come for its usual hay,
stared dumbfounded where the strange bundle lay.

Handfuls of straw, meant for the sheep,
pillowed the young Lamb of God's first sleep.

And all the shy insects in his manger spoke
when with strong human cry the Infant awoke.

Theophany
(Luke 2 & Matthew 1–2)

What are we who tried so hard
to keep you far from us,
addressing you as God Most High,
Lord, King, and offering gold on gold,
clouds of incense, myrrh,
to make of this?

What are we who tried so hard
to save you from the smell
of those below the bottom rung
and now must step around still steaming
dung to reach your manger bed
to make of this?

What are we who tried so hard
to pick and purchase gifts of royal ilk
and now see you, despite malodorous
incense, drafty cold, move toward
your mother's milk with infant bliss
to make of this?

Jew-El

(LUKE 2:25–32)

As Simeon walked with wisdom and age
down the temple corridor, his eyes,
searching through candlelight,
dimly told him of a woman waiting,
her body wrapped with reverent joy
around her infant son.

He bent to receive the small Jew (the small
Jewel set in a brooch of mothering arms),
and his beard, touching,
tingled like telegraph wires
telling the good news:
What hath God wrought!

Old eyes saw an infinite Light,
old hands cradled the face,
grace poured.
No one spoke till
"Now," his old voice broke,
"you may dismiss your servant, Lord."

FIRST WORD

Mary stirred a measure of flour
into the leaven and listened to Jesus
giggle and coo through the sounds of languages
living and dead. She laughed as she added
a second cup to the bubbling batter—
for all she knew, her son could be babbling
in Greek.

She added a third measure, worked it
into the glutinous mass, and added
a fourth. As she scraped the sides of the bowl,
she remembered the scrape of the olive tree
against her father's house while she listened,
inside, to words more foreign than any
her son was speaking now.

She was up to her wrists in the sticky dough
when Jesus arrived at the initial sounds
of their native tongue. She flew from kitchen
to carpenter shop, floured her husband's
hand midway between awl and hammer,
and ran back with him.

Their cradled son, his fingers and toes
curling around the olive wood rattle
that Joseph had lately carved for him,
was distinctly repeating the Aleph and Beth
of his native tongue to the leavening dough
and spellbound table and chairs:
"Abba, Abba, Abba."

LITANY FOR ORDINARY TIME

Mary, queen of the ordinary—
    queen of spinning wheel and loom
        who wove from ordinary stuff
        the flawless fabric of
        God's humanness;

    queen whose pregnancy
        put Joseph's other plans aside
        and sent his saw singing
        into cradle wood;

    queen of water jars daily filled,
        of swaddling clothes spread outdoors
        to dry, of scrubbed floors
        and everlastingly sawdusty son;

    queen of skinned knees,
        splintered fingers,
        aching stomach, fevered head,
        herbal teas;

    queen of fresh-baked bread
        whose wheaty power
        put flesh on growing boy
        and joy at evening meal—

Mary, queen of ordinary time and space,
thank you for your ordinary grace.

GROWING PAINS
(LUKE 2:42–50)

That day
when they finally found him
after looking high and low,
and Mary asked in hurt surprise,
"Why, child?" and heard him say,
"But Mother, didn't you know
I had to stay?"
and saw the pleading eyes
(*When the Father calls,*
I cannot not obey!)
of her growing son,
Mary came to realize
the pain of bearing him
had just begun.

Mary Pondered All These Things

(Luke 2:50–52)

She had no words to express
her feelings of awe and loss
after their return from Jerusalem,
as she watched the boy Jesus
tear himself tenderly but firmly away,
though he still obeyed them.

She had always known
she did not own him.
Yet his words to her in the Temple
when she and Joseph found him
after searching three days
were seared in her heart with live coals.

Mornings now she brought him
to her heart's Temple and offered him.
Evenings she stood at the door
and welcomed him home again.
At supper she watched him
eat like every other hungry boy.

She knew this life in Nazareth would end;
how soon, she did not know.
Each day she taught the young Son of God
how to wait and trust.
Each day she plumbed new depths
of letting go.

III

"YOU ARE MY BELOVED SON"

JOHN THE BAPTIST: THE PASSOVER
(JOHN 1:35–39)

For years he'd preached the coming was at hand.
Now John saw Jesus walking on the strand.
"Behold the Lamb of God!" he called, and sent
his own disciples hurrying. They went,
filling Jesus' footprints in the sand
faster than the water could. John stayed and poured
the river on the people and passed them over to his Lord.

BELOVED SON
(MARK 1:9–11)

The waters broke
and Jesus rose—
the Anointed One.

Clouds tore asunder,
winged words flew
to this Noah-Ark,
this Earth washed new.

"You are my beloved Son!"
God spoke
in glorious thunder.

THE TESTING (A TRIPTYCH)

(LUKE 4:1–13)

. . . who, though he was in the form of God,
did not regard equality with God
as something to be exploited,
but emptied himself . . . (PHILIPPIANS 2:6–8)

1. LOAVES OF STONE

Watching the slant light of morning
finger the stones of the wall he had built
to shelter himself from cold night winds,
he sensed that before the sun had burned out

on the other end of the wilderness,
the trials would show their evil faces.
Filled with dread, he got up from his mat
and knelt to beg for strength to endure.

Words at last washed over him:
"Have no fear. I am with you.
I myself will tell you what to say!"
He arose, refreshed, ready.

Hunger seized him—an alien creature
gnawing his insides, engorging itself,
snaking up from the pit of his stomach
into his chest, his throat, his mouth.

At arm's reach, the top row of stones
glowed smooth and round as the loaves
his mother had baked and set on the shelf
to cool when he was a growing boy.

A thought padded into his mind,
mewed around and around his senses.
"If you are the Son of God," it purred,
"try out your 'Abba, cadabra.'

"If you asked the Father for bread,
would he give you a stone?"
Its tongue searched the hollows
of his hunger, exquisitely licking, licking.
Bewildered, Jesus looked at the stones.
On the morning of the world
they had tumbled forth from God's mouth
to be building blocks, not bread.

They had sheltered him
and would shelter others after him—
unless, to placate his hunger,
he made them pawns of his power.

He would not do it.
"One does not live by bread alone,"
he said with finality, "but by every word
that comes from the mouth of God."

Hunger snarled, but slithered away.

2. The Reign of God

Higher and yet higher he was led
till all the kingdoms of the world lay spread
before his eyes, more splendid still
than he had ever dreamed.
"Worship me and these are yours,"
the Tempter said.

Mountains boomed and echoed
a thundering "No!"

The Son of Man would choose instead to go
where he was sent, to have no place
to lay his head, to be content
to spread himself cross-beamed
above a common hill.

3. FROM THE PINNACLE

From the temple's height he saw pilgrims
streaming down Judean hills, surging up
the Cedron valley, pouring through
the city gates, swirling toward the temple.
The sacred stairs below him jammed
with flotsam and jetsam.
A sweet-sour stench steamed up
of burning wool, feathers, incense.

The Tempter's breath seared Jesus' ear:
"The people have come to renew the covenant
with the One who promised a Messiah.
If you are the Son of God,
throw yourself down that they may know it.
For it is written, 'He will command his angels
concerning you,' and 'They will bear you up
lest you dash your foot against a stone.'"

In his fantasy Jesus saw himself leap
from the ledge of his humanness—Yahweh's darling
defying the laws of ordinary flesh,
plummeting down toward the terrified crowd,
then caught and enthroned on seraphic wings.
From there he swung like a golden censer
pouring down blessings on pilgrims who came,
year after year, to adore him.

Was this the leap of faith the Spirit was urging?

Through a blur of incense, he recognized faces
of friends and neighbors from Galilee
whose tables and chairs he had made and mended.
When the people returned to their fields and flocks,
planting and harvesting, washing and baking,
lovemaking and childbearing,
what good would it do them to know
the Messiah awaited their yearly worship?

Who would walk with them
in the winter seasons
and in that sunless valley
where there are no reasons?

"Leave me," he thundered. "Again it is written,
'Do not put the Lord your God to the test.'"

Even as the Evil One slunk away,
Jesus knew they would one day meet again.

IV

"BEHOLD, I COME TO DO YOUR WILL"

CANA WINE
(JOHN 2:1–11)

"The weather's so hot
and no more wine's to be bought
in all of Cana!
It's just what I feared—
just why I begged my husband
to keep the wedding small."

"Does he know?" Mary asked.

"Not yet. Oh, the shame!
Look at my son and his beautiful bride!
They'll never be able
to raise their heads again,
not in this small town."

"Then don't tell him yet."

Mary greeted the guests
as she made her way
through crowded reception rooms.
"I must talk to you, Son,"
she said unobtrusively.

Moments later he moved
toward the back serving rooms.
They hadn't seen each other
since the morning he'd left her—
before the baptism
and the desert time.

There was so much to tell her,
so much to ask.
But this was not the time!
They could talk tomorrow
on the way to Capernaum.

She spoke urgently, her words
both request and command to him:
"They have no wine."
But he hadn't been called yet!
He hadn't felt it yet.
Would she send him so soon
to the hounds and jackals?
For wine?

Was wine so important then?

"Woman, what concern is that
to you and me?
My hour has not yet come."

Her unflinching eyes reflected to him
his twelve-year-old self
telling her with no contrition:
"Why were you searching for me?
Did you not know I must be
in my Father's house?"

She left him standing there—
vine from her stock,
ready for fruit bearing—
and went to the servants.
"Do whatever he tells you," she said.

From across the room
she watched them fill water jars,
watched the chief steward
drink from the dripping cup,
saw his eyes open in wide surprise.

She watched her grown son
toast the young couple,
watched the groom's parents
and the guests raise their cups.

She saw it all clearly:
saw the Best Wine
pouring out for them all.

HEALING OF THE PARALYTIC
(MARK 2:1–12)

There were some who insisted
that Jacob's paralysis
was punishment for his secret sins
and he wasn't worth our pity.
But when we heard about the leper
who showed up healed by Jesus,
we four got together.
"There ought to be a way," we said,
"to help Jacob, too."

When we got to Jesus' place,
the crowd wouldn't let us through,
what with the mat and all.
"Why not try the roof?"
someone said, laughing.
We looked at each other.
We'd come too far for nothing.
"Let's try it!" we said.

We edged around the crowd
to the back of the house,
hoisted up the litter and Jacob,
and poked a hole in the thatch.
The oily voices of Jerusalem scribes,
heckling Jesus, seeped up to us.
"Let's give the Master a break," we said,
and tore the roof apart.

We lowered the mat
and swung ourselves down
in a rain of dust and straw.
The scribes sputtered and coughed
into gold-embroidered sleeves
and retreated to the corners.
But Jesus smiled us a welcome,
brushed the straw from his shoulders,
and turned his eyes toward Jacob.
The room watched in silence
as the Master leaned down to touch him.
"Your sins are forgiven," he said.
As rumbling rose from the shadows,
Jesus' command rang clear:
"Stand up! Take your bed and go home!"

Jacob sprang up like a wheat stalk
and carried his mat out the door.

We stayed to listen to Jesus
as he shone in a shaft of light,
the dust we had raised
forming an aura around him.

STORM AT SEA
(MARK 4:37–41)

All chaos broke loose
from the bottom of the sea!
At first I didn't want to wake him
to the demons shrieking
below, above, and all around us.

Let him sleep, I thought—
there were no extra oars
and no more buckets
for bailing.
Why wake him to the terror?

But when I saw demonic faces
leering from the waves above us,
ready to crunch and devour
our cockleshell of boat,
I needed him to be with us.

One touch and he was awake,
looking at me in guileless surprise,
waiting for me to explain why I woke him.
The wind ripped my words to shreds:
"Master! We are drowning!"

Immediately, Jesus arose to full height
and commanded the sea, "Peace! Be still!"
The demons wailed in agony
and retreated to the deep.
The wind lay quiet as a sleeping cat.

"Why were you afraid?" he chided.
"Have you still no faith?"
We rowed back in awed silence,
wondering: *Who is this then*
that even the wind and the sea obey him?

Gerasene Demoniac
(Mark 5:1–20)

Shrieks and cackles split the air
as we neared the beach of the Gerasenes.
We begged to turn back, but Jesus set
his face like flint and said to go in.
Even before we could dock the boat,
he plunged through the sand and ran up the trail
toward the burial grounds.

We scrambled up after him.
Rocks big as water jars hurtled down toward us.
Above, at the summit, a naked creature,
mouth foaming, chains clanging,
scuttled from tomb to tomb, screaming,
"What do you have to do with me,
Jesus, Son of the Most High God?"

We heard the Master demand its name.
"Legion," it howled, whining for mercy.
The next thing we knew, two thousand swine
rushed down past us and into the sea.
When all was quiet, we walked up the hill.
The Gerasene sat at Jesus' feet,
fully clothed, his chains beside him.

Herdsmen came running from neighboring hills.
Their countryman's healing went unnoticed
as they lamented the loss of their swine and implored us
to leave their land. When we got to our boat
the Gerasene begged for permission to join us.
But Jesus told him, "Go home. Tell your friends
what the Lord has done for you."

We talked among ourselves late that evening.
Clearly, the Master had power beyond Galilee.
Even in pagan lands, the demons obeyed him.
Already, we disciples were a motley mix
of fishers and tax collectors, men and women.
What would we have done if Jesus had invited
the Gentile to join us? Would that time ever come?

HOMECOMING
(MARK 6:1–4)

A tiger sea,
its foaming jaws ready
to tear boat and fishermen
caught in its claws,
turned kitten-tame
and lay at his feet.

Unclean spirits
stormed from their victims,
loudly protesting
their furious witness:
"What do you want of us,
Holy One of God?"

But Nazarene neighbors
faithfully clung
to their wide reputation
of narrow meanness
and ran their carpenter-son
out of town.

ECSTASY'S END

(MARK 9:5–8)

We wanted to stay
on Tabor's height
to shout
Alleluia
all day,
every day.

But the light
went out.

LIKE A LITTLE CHILD:
A STORY IN TWO VOICES
(MARK 10:14–16)

The Disciples:
>Be like a child?
>like a sniveling child picking at its nose?
>like a chicken following a clucking hen?
>like this thumb-sucking child?

>He's not married—he's never been
>awakened by a squalling kid who can't say
>what it wants and so you have to guess.
>He wants us to imitate such helplessness?

Jesus:
>Bless you, child, little miracle
>of bone and flesh as soft as flower petals!
>Child so new, your mother's love
>still clings like summer dew!

>Her hands, warm against your back,
>are telling you to trust me.
>See—
>she lets me hold your hand.

>God's love is like your mother's, child.
>You can't earn it, but you *can*
>pass on this lesson
>as you learn to be a man.

BLIND TRUST
(MARK 10:46–52)

Bartimaeus sat outside
the town of Jericho.
The more they told him where to go,
the louder he cried.

He had no pride—
when Jesus asked, he simply stated:
"Lord, I want to see!" and waited
to be eyed.

Firstborn Sons and the Widow of Nain

(Luke 7:11–15)

Jesus halted on the road outside Nain
where a woman's wailing drenched the air.
Out of the gates poured a somber procession
of dark-shawled women, hushed children,
young men bearing a litter that held
a body swathed in burial clothes,
and the woman, walking alone.

> *A widow then—another bundle*
> *of begging rags at the city gates.*
> *A bruised reed!*

Her loud grief labored and churned in him till
"Halt!" he shouted.

The crowd, the woman, the dead man stopped.
Dust, raised by sandaled feet,
settled down again on the sandy road.
Insects waited in shocked silence.

He walked to the litter, grasped a dead hand.
"Young man," he called
in a voice that shook the walls of Sheol,
"I command you, rise!"

The linens stirred.
Two firstborn sons from Nazareth and Nain
met, eye to eye.

He placed the pulsing hand into hers.
"Woman, behold your son," he smiled.

"She Has Shown Great Love"
(Luke 7:36–50)

When she learned where Jesus had gone,
the woman raced home,
grabbed scarves and jewels,
ran to pawn them,
bought the biggest jar of nard she could buy,
and flew to the house of Simon the Pharisee.

In the doorway she stopped to catch her breath
and to let her eyes adjust to the dark.
The room was filled with men,
some of whom had known her more than once.
She felt lewd eyes undressing her again.
But then she saw Jesus.

Those others didn't matter anymore.
In a second she was on the floor,
breaking open the alabaster jar,
pouring out the nard, anointing his ankles,
his hard soles, his long straight toes,
kissing them, wiping them with her hair.

Only then did she remember the Law—
by touching him, she had made him unclean!
Self-loathing sobbed in her as she saw herself
groveling for bread when she was too young
for her woman's trade, and later, being tossed
like a toy, devoured quickly in the dark.

She felt his quiet hand on her head,
heard him speaking to his host,
"Simon, I have something to say to you."
She poured out more oil, slowly, deliberately,
held the jar upside down and poured it all out,
her tears falling all the while unto his feet.

"Do you see this woman?" Jesus continued.
"She has shown great love."
When she dared look up to him,
his kind eyes anointed her from head to foot.
"Your sins are forgiven," he solemnly assured her.
"Your faith has saved you; go in peace."

She wiped the excess oil from between his toes,
stood up and left the room, carrying with her
the fragrance of forgiveness.

FAITH POWER
(LUKE 8:43-48)

She did not want to make him unclean,
but Jesus would never have to know.
She would just touch the fringe of his garments
and go.

In that noisy sea of anonymity,
her hand flew, withdrew
again. She heard him say,
"Someone touched me! Who? Who?"

A disciple laughed, "Master, in this crowd
you were touched by everyone!"
But when he insisted, "I felt power
going out of me," she flung herself down.

"It was I!" she confessed and, trembling, told
her bloody story out loud, despite her fears—
the killing doctor bills, the twelve unclean,
untouchable years.

Jesus proclaimed her healing
to the whole astounded street:
"Daughter, your faith has made you well!"
and raised her to her feet.

When a Little Was Enough
(Luke 9:10–17)

"Send the people away from this deserted place
to find food and lodgings," the twelve urged Jesus,
"for the day is advanced and it is almost evening."

Jesus looked at the crowd (there were about five
thousand)
and looked at his disciples, still excited and tired
from their first mission journey.

What had they learned from the villagers of Galilee
who shared bread and sheltered them from cold night
winds?
What had they learned of human coldness on the way?

He remembered the pain in his mother's voice
as she told of his birth night when they found no room
in all of Bethlehem, House of Bread.

"*You* give them something to eat!" he said.

"We have only five loaves and two fish!" they protested.
"How can we feed so many with so little?"
He understood their incredulity.

They had yet to learn that a little was enough
when it was all they had—
that God could turn these very stones to bread.

"Have the crowd sit down in groups of fifty," he said.
Jesus took the food and looked up to heaven.
He blessed it, broke it, gave it to the disciples
to distribute to the new-formed churches.

Afterwards, when everyone was satisfied,
the twelve filled twelve baskets of bread left over—
as faith stirred like yeast within them.

BETHANY DECISIONS
(LUKE 10:38–42)

As Jesus taught the gathered brothers
and Martha boiled and baked their dinner,
Mary eavesdropped in the anteroom
between the great hall and the kitchen.
Her dying mother's warning words
clanged clearly in her memory—
"Obey your sister. She has learned
the ways and duties of a woman."

She'd learned her sister's lessons well
and knew a woman's place was *not*
to sit and listen and be taught.
But when she heard the voice of Jesus
call to her above the din
of Martha's boiling pots and pans,
she made her choice decisively—
took off her apron and traditions,
and walked in.

WOMAN UN-BENT
(LUKE 13:10–17)

That Sabbath day as always
she went to the synagogue
and took the place assigned her
right behind the grill where,
the elders had concurred,
she would block no one's view,
she could lean her heavy head,
and (though this was not said)
she'd give a good example to
the ones who stood behind her.

That day, intent as always
on the Word (for eighteen years
she'd listened thus), she heard
Authority when Jesus spoke.

Though long stripped
of forwardness,
she came forward, nonetheless,
when Jesus summoned her.

"Woman, you are free
of your infirmity," he said.

The leader of the synagogue
worked himself into a sweat
as he tried to bend the Sabbath
and the woman back in place.

But she stood up straight and let
God's glory touch her face.

JESUS PREACHES FROM THE BOAT
(MARK 4:1–2; LUKE 12:22–31,15)

From where he sat in Peter's boat,
feet in the water, face aglow,
Jesus told us parables
of weeds in wheat, mustard seed,

of a lost sheep, a lost coin,
a lost son found—
of friends and neighbors called each time
to share the finder's joy.

Above the lake gulls circled,
plummeted to make a catch;
plovers skittered down the beach,
warblers foraged in the weeds.

"Look at the birds," Jesus said.
"How tenderly God feeds them!
How splendidly the flowers bloom!
God loves you more than these."

Standing on the beach that morning
drinking in the Master's stories
in the midst of friends and neighbors,
I felt the joy of heaven.

The Lost Parable
(Luke 15:3–10)

Luke placed the lost coin beside the lost sheep—
in parallel stories that show God's love
for every lost one of us.

Thus:
> *"What man among you,*
> *having a hundred sheep*
> *and losing one of them . . .*
>> *"Or what woman*
>> *having ten coins*
>> *and losing one . . .*
> *"would not . . . go after the lost one*
> *until he finds it?*
>> *"would not . . . search carefully*
>> *until she finds it?*
> *"And when he does find it, . . .*
> *he calls together*
> *his friends and neighbors . . .*
>> *"And when she does find it,*
>> *she calls together*
>> *her friends and neighbors . . .*
> *"and says to them, 'Rejoice with me*
> *for I have found my lost sheep.'"*
>> *"and says to them, 'Rejoice with me*
>> *for I have found the coin I lost.'"*

"In just the same way," Luke's Jesus concludes,
"his joy and hers are like the joy found in heaven
when a sinner returns."

Since the stories were written, hundreds of artists
have rescued lost lambs from their hazardous heights
by cradling them in the Good Shepherd's arms.
But the coin is still stuck in the cracks! Who will find it?

Who but a homemaker will sweep all the floors,
search drawers and shelves from attic to basement,
turn the house upside-down, and never give up
till her broom uncovers the dust from the drachma!

When she has found it and calls us all in
to rejoice with her, may we see at last
whose image it bears—
how the silver coin shines in the light of her eyes!
how it catches the glints of the silvery hair
of that Good Homemaker rejoicing in heaven!

Father and Son: Two Prodigals

(Luke 15:12–24)

Envy like fermenting yeast
swelled and choked him as he watched
the squealing beasts shove filthy snouts
into heaping troughs of grain.

He, a Jew, jealous of pigs!
It was time, he knew, to go home.

Though shame and dread tried to turn him back,
hunger goaded him on the thirsty road
until he reached the summit of the last hill
as the third day stumbled into evening.

In the valley below he saw olive trees blooming,
ewes and their lambs bleating in the sheepfold,
a long line of cattle plodding toward the barns,
young calves cavorting around their mothers . . .

and there—could it be his father watched for him?—
a man came running up the path!

He fell to his knees and began his practiced speech.
But when he reached the "Let-me-be-your-slave" part,
his father raised him, embraced him,
repeatedly named him: "My son, my son!"

Slaves were sent racing to bring the best robe,
sandals for his feet, and a ring for his finger.
"Then fetch the fatted calf! We'll feast tonight,
for my son who was lost has come home!"

Nothing, he knew, could earn such forgiveness.
Yet in the years to come
there was hard work to do—
he must grow to be such a father's son.

JESUS AND ZACCHAEUS: A SHORT STORY
(LUKE 19:1–10)

Too short to see,
Zacchaeus climbed a tree.

Most folks wouldn't give tuppence
for such comeuppance,

but when Jesus saw him
far out on a limb,

he called to that sinner,
"Come down and make dinner."

Zacchaeus gave away
all his ill-gotten pay.
He grew tall that day.

Encounter with the Canaanite Woman
(Matthew 15:21–28)

The Canaanite woman, interrupting the company's
retreat by the sea, shouted in deep distress,
"Have mercy on me, Lord, Son of David,
my daughter is tormented by a demon!"
But he did not answer her at all.

When the disciples (faithful sons of the House
of Israel, who had left everything to follow him)
urged him to "Send her away, for she keeps
shouting after us," he told her, "I was sent
only to the lost sheep of the House of Israel."

What was the tone of his words? the intent?
Were they meant to thunder her into silence?
Was he following dictates definitively taught
by the scribes (Thou shalt not talk to Gentiles.
Thou shalt not talk in public to women.)?

Was it his tiredness, the heat, the light searing
off the sand, the awareness that what she was asking
was no mere miracle, but a vast hurricane of events
that would send the House of Israel reeling off the rock
where it had stood for a millennium and more

which prompted him to answer her plea with
"It is not fair to take the children's food and throw it
to the dogs"—words congruent with the tradition
that had caused the Israelite fathers to cleanse the tribe
by sending their pagan wives whining back to Canaan?

Or was he trying to probe the depth of the mother lode—
the faith of a mother who, faced with her daughter's
     dying,
had sent her own fearsome demons flying?
She knelt at his feet—this woman from the coast—
as her wise brothers from the East had done long ago

when they finally found him in his mother's arms,
blissfully content and unaware of their homage.
Did her womb-love plumb the unfathomable well
of his own compassion (Hath not a Gentile eyes, hands,
organs, dimensions, senses, affections, passions)?
Could it be that she, by the faith and force
of her wit—"Yes Lord, yet even the dogs
eat the crumbs that fall from their master's table"—
crumbled the unpalatable crusts of the fathers
and showed him it was right and just

to pull the tablecloth down, spread it out
on the sand (How endlessly it stretched—
a white field to harvest!)
for Jews and Gentiles, sons and daughters
to sit and feast together beside healing waters?

EXPANDING THE MISSION
(MATTHEW 15:21–28)

Jesus planned their day of R & R
carefully. He led his followers to a far
seashore to avoid the usual needy crowd.
But there a Canaanite woman came with loud
persistent shout
until he had to listen, had to hear her out.

When finally he understood her urgent matter
(She wanted him to heal her dying daughter!),
he told her there was nothing he could do
for her: she wasn't family, wasn't a Jew.
It was to them alone that he was sent.
Doggedly, she squelched that argument

and would not quit until he saw a wider mission:
Would his good God not set aside a tired tradition
dividing race and class and creeds
to tend an innocent child's needs?
"Family" includes the dogs, not only those who sit
at table. He saw her point, marveled at her wit,

and did a human-Godly thing—
he gave her dying child a spring.

DISCIPLESHIP
(MATTHEW 16:21–24)

Resolute,
you turn your face
toward Jerusalem,
tell us you must go
and why you must.

Fearfully,
I follow you
with slow
slow pace,
dry as dust.

AT JACOB'S WELL (A TRIPTYCH)
(JOHN 4:4–42)

1. EXCHANGE

"Please," he repeated, "I'm thirsty.
Give me a drink." The words
hung in the air between them
like a hand extended in peace.

Shocked, distrustful, she seized
her only weapon. "You people,"
she spat, "think we're nothing but scum.
Here's a cupful of scum if you want it."

He drank her bitter face.
"If you knew the gift of God," he began,
probing her arid soul
with careful divining rod.

They sat and talked for a spell.
She gave him a cup of water.
He gave her a well.

2. RECONCILIATION

He watched as she came up
the path to the well. The apple
of noonday sun hung heavy
and ripe on Mount Gerezim.

He had watched Abraham,
with Sarah, swear the covenant
and build his altar
on the mountain's heights

and had watched their children's children,
still trumpeting Jericho's fall,
return to renew the covenant
at the altar of the mountain.

He had watched and waited
for generations and generations
as the tribes wandered again.
He was tired and thirsty from waiting.

"Woman, give me a drink,"
he begged, shattering to shards
the laws dividing Jew from Samaritan,
men from women, clean from unclean.

"How can you, a Jew, ask a woman
of Samaria for a drink?" she scolded,
parrying his peacemaking
with her empty cup.

"Woman, broken by broken covenants,"
he said, "leave these man-made
laws and buckets. Take the truth
of Living Water, springing up inside you,

"and carry it to your people.
Tell them the prophet they wait for—
the I AM who told you everything—
is waiting for them at the well."

After her telling, all Samaria
came out to drink his words.
The black sheep of Israel
grew fat again on the flowing hills.

Joseph rested at last in peace
at the well of his father Jacob.
And in her burial cave in Hebron,
Sarah's brittle bones dissolved in laughter.

3. To Jesus at the Well

Midnight Dew,
grown now to
dayspring, waiting in
parched noon for woman
to bring her heavy jars
to draw water from a tired well,

teach her
to seek wells
beyond her dreaming—
to leave battered buckets at
dead cisterns and clean the debris
from the living spring inside her.

Christ, guide her to that flowing sea.

WOMAN TAKEN IN ADULTERY
(JOHN 8:2–11)

From the angry crunch of their sandaled feet
as they left the courtyard, Jesus knew,
without looking up from his writing on the ground,
that the Pharisees and scribes still carried their stones.

The woman stood where they'd shoved her,
her hair hanging loose over neck and face,
her hands still shielding her head
from the stones she awaited.

"Woman," he asked, "has no one condemned you?"

The heap of woman shuddered, unfolded.
She viewed the courtyard—empty now—
with wild, glazed eyes and turned back to him.
"No one, Sir," she said, unsurely.

Compassion flooded him like a wadi after rain.
He thought of his mother—had she known such fear?—
and of the gentle man whom he had called *Abba*.
Only when Joseph lay dying had he confided
his secret anguish on seeing his betrothed
swelling up with seed not his own.

"Neither do I condemn you," Jesus said.
"Go your way and sin no more."

Black eyes looked out from an ashen face,
empty, uncomprehending.
Then life rushed back.
She stood before him like a blossoming tree.

"Go in peace and sin no more,"
Jesus called again as she left the courtyard.

He had bought her at a price, he knew.
The stony hearts of her judges
would soon hurl their hatred at him.
His own death was a mere stone's throw away.

RETURN OF LAZARUS
(JOHN 11:39–44)

A mighty Wind breaks through the stony
walls of Sheol, transports me
to the mortal dwelling I once knew,
searches every corner of the empty
house, and breathes me into it again.

I wake to darkness and the smell
of death and myrrh, find my flesh
bound to bone by burial shroud.
A Voice commands, "Lazarus, come forth!"
Obediently, I stumble through

death's shattered door. Outside,
my sisters, friends, and neighbors
bear witness to my rising,
their mouths unhinged, their eyes
round with startled awe and fear.

A Man with recent tears
still drying on his face commands:
"Unbind him and let him go!"
I know the Voice, kneel, adore
the Master of my death and life.

ANOINTINGS IN BETHANY
(JOHN 12:1–8)

Solemnly, Mary entered the room,
holding high the alabaster jar.
It gleamed in the lamplight as she circled the room,
incensing the disciples, blessing Martha's banquet.
"A splendid table!" Mary called with her eyes
as she whirled past her sister.

She came to a halt at last before Jesus,
bowed profoundly and knelt at his feet.
Defily, she filled her right hand with nard,
placed the jar on the floor,
took one foot in her hands
and moved fragrant fingers across his instep.

Over and over she made the journey
from heel to toes, thanking him
for every step he had made
on Judea's stony hills,
for every stop at their home,
for bringing back Lazarus.

She poured out more nard,
took his other foot in her hands
and started again with strong, rhythmic strokes.
She felt her hands' heat draw out his tiredness,
take away the rebuffs he had known—
the shut doors, the shut hearts.

Energy flowed like a river between them.
His saturated skin gleamed with oil.

But she had no towel!

In an instant she pulled off her veil,
pulled the pins from her hair,
shook it out till it fell in cascades
and once more cradled each foot,
dried the ankles, the insteps,
drew the strands between his toes.

Without warning, Judas Iscariot
spat out his anger, the words hissing
like lightning above her unveiled head:
"Why was this perfume not sold
for three hundred denarii
and the money given to the poor?"

"Leave her alone!"
Jesus silenced the usurper.
"She bought it so that she might keep it
for the day of my burial."

The words poured like oil,
anointing her from head to foot.

V

"INTO YOUR HANDS
I COMMEND MY SPIRIT"

ENTRY INTO JERUSALEM
(MARK 11:1-9)

Like a king he came,
astride a steed adorned with regal cloak,
to receive the crowd's acclaim:
"Hosanna! Blessed be the Name
of the Lord!"

But it was a gentle joke—
his prancing horse a borrowed colt,
jittery in the crowd,
ready to bolt back home
with all its purple rags.

Before he turned the people's
messianic hopes
completely upside down,
he rode into Jerusalem
majestic as a clown.

Overturning Tables: Reclaiming the Temple
(Matthew 21:12-16)

Hosannas still rang in the cobblestoned streets
as Jesus reached the temple, mounted the steps.
Marketplace bedlam assaulted his senses:
pilgrims, bewildered, milled around tables where
money changers, dove sellers conspired to ensnare them.
Caged doves and pigeons flew in frenzied circles.

Jesus watched a young laborer lay down his coins—
three month's wages—at one of the tables,
heard the pride in his voice singing out "for a son,"
saw his face turn scarlet as he desperately dug
for more coins to purchase the currency he needed
to buy two turtle doves and two young pigeons.

The unfair extortion was too much for Jesus.
His voice a whip, he lashed at the money changers,
the dove sellers too—the whole conniving lot of them—
overturned tables, freed the birds, smashed cages.
"You have made my house of prayer a den of thieves!" he
    shouted.
They fled from his wrath, lugging their purses.

It was a coup de grace! Priests watched in horror
as cripples crawled up the steps, the blind close behind
    them—
the unclean *anawim* reclaiming the temple.
The doves he had freed hovered over Jesus.
Behold the Lamb of God, they sang,
come to pay the price for all.

In the streets below, children still sang hosannas.

LEGACY
(MATTHEW 26:26–28)

When he was a child
his mother told him
of how she and Joseph
had been turned away
from their ancestral home—
the House of Bread—
on the night of his birth.

The story taught him
that rejection and hunger
gnawed with the same teeth.

Grown, he walked through
towns and countryside,
feeding hollow-eyed hundreds
who pursued him by day.
But a bottomless ocean
of hungry mouths
flooded his dreams.

He learned that the memory
of yesterday's bread
could not relieve today's hunger.

On the eve of his death,
he at last found a way
to keep rejection and hunger
at bay. He held his life in his hands
and said to his friends,
"Take. Eat. This is my body,
broken for you."

And when they were filled, commanded:
"Feed the hungry. Do this.
Re-member me."

Last Lesson
(John 13:3–16)

The festive table glowed with candles,
warding off the darkness lurking
in the corners of the upper room.

As soon as we had found a place,
for once not quarreling over who
sat next to Jesus, he removed
his outer robe, wrapped a towel
around himself, poured a basin
full of water, and knelt at Peter's feet!

"Lord," he blurted, "you shall never
wash my feet!" Jesus warned him:
"If you do not let me wash you,
you can have no share with me."
Poor Peter begged, "Then wash my hands
and head as well." But Jesus answered:

"Those who bathe need only have
their feet washed." We sat embarrassed,
listening to the water splash.
Still on his knees, the Master looked
at us then. "You are clean,"
he added, "though not all of you."

And so we let him wash our feet!
Afterwards, he questioned, "Do you
understand what I have done?"

Our hopes of glory gone, we sat
in silence. He went on: "You call me
Lord and Teacher. You are right.
Tonight I, your Lord and Teacher,
have set you an example: Do
for one another as I have done."

The supper table glowed with candles
warding off the crouching darkness
as we—his chosen servant leaders—
listened to our Master Teacher
nailing down his final lesson
on the night before he died.

And It Was Night
(John 13:30)

You stumble unseeing from the upper room,
and no number of lanterns and torches can dim
your darkness now, Judas. When did you let
the light go out? When did you begin
to guard the hoard and spend starry evenings
behind drawn tent flaps, counting coins
with acquisitive fingers while the company sat
together outside at a crackling campfire,
breaking bread and talking of Light?

When did you fine-tune your ears to the clink
of copper and silver and gold, letting
the words of the Master fade out unheeded?
When did you start to begrudge begging hands
and when did you welcome disciples more
for the treasures they gave than the treasures they were?

Now, in the dark of Gethsemane's garden,
you touch greedy lips to the Master's cheek—
a cheap giveaway to your cohorts of night.

MOUNT OF OLIVES
(LUKE 22:41–44)

He falls, crying,
"Help me, Father."
Though his acquiescence rings
true as a well-tuned violin,

the searing bow brings
tears of blood
as it plays across the taut strings
of his human dread of dying.

AGONY
(LUKE 22:41–44)

Lo!
Who is this lying
in the shadowed
garden—

this human, shivering Plea,
this caught-between-
the-Agony-
and-Dying,

this (dear God, no!)
crushed
Christ
crying!

BETRAYAL
(LUKE 22:54–62)

Peter, so quick to say
you'd take the devil by the tail
and give him hell to pay,

so ready with your sword,
so sure,
so strong—

did not the Lord himself
call you his rock,
and could he be wrong?

Now the cock crows
and you, cocksure rock,
implode to emptiness.

Stabat Mater

I stand with every mother
at the roadsides of the world
to watch my child struggle
up the hill.

I taught my little boy to walk
and set him on his feet again
each time he fell, until he learned
to walk alone.

He's grown and gone beyond me now
and nothing's left for me to do
except to follow close behind him
on the way.

When his feet go out from under him,
I can no longer lift him up,
but I have taught him how
to rise again.

Jesus Comforts the Women
(Luke 23:27–28)

Even as we cried for him,
he tried to console us.

"Dear friends, I'll be all right,"
he said, as blood spurted
from beneath the thorns.
"I can see the end now.
But you must be strong.
Your passion is yet to come."

When his voice caught,
choking on sweat and blood
that rivered down his face,
we cried afresh
as we tried to assure him
we'd be all right.

THE NAILING
(MARK 15:24)

Stand tall, soldier, be a man!
You are the chosen one.
Do your duty for the State.
Let Caesar's will be done!

Hit the nail right on the head.
Nail this King of the Jews.
Let your hammering be heard
wherever treason brews.

Nail him down with all your force.
Nail him down good.
Let them see his feet and fingers
twitch against the wood.

Miss the nail once or twice.
Hit him where he bleeds.
Make his body paint the way
to where sedition leads.

Tell them by each hammer blow
that Rome will last forever.
No power on earth can overthrow
Caesar's power, never!

Now your men can raise the cross.
Your bloody work is done.
The King of Jews is crucified.
Rome is Number One.

THE GAME
(JOHN 19:23–25)

"So fine a tunic it would be
a crime to tear," they said
and shot their dice instead
beneath the cross.

Afterwards,
when he had died
they tore a hole into his side,
considering it no loss.

CRUCIFIXION
(MARK 15:25–37)

Stripped of godliness,
hands hammered open,
arms yanked wide,
the cross-beamed Christ
pours himself out
till rivers run red with
wine enough to satisfy
century-cries of thirst.

MANY WOMEN WERE ALSO THERE

(MARK 15:25–41)

Their friend was hanging on the cross.
They were at a total loss
for ways to help him—clearly knew
that there was nothing they could do.

Obscene hecklers leered at them.
Passers-by jeered at them:
"Some King you've got up there—some clown!"
They could not—would not—let him down.

The women simply, strongly stood
loving him beneath the wood.

PIETÀ

The Sabbath hush
has stilled the rush
of the crucifying.
I'm numb with dying.
And could my tears
give more years
to my dead Son?

Yet even now
I know, somehow,
as they un-nail him
limb by limb
from the tree
and give him back to me,
that mothering goes on and on.

VI

"HE IS RISEN. . . .
GO TELL THE OTHERS"

PASCHAL PARADOX

flower of salvation
from soil of creation

Christ Jesus rising, cross bearing fruit
white-petalled flower, red stem and root
Now of yesterday, Now of tomorrow
birth from death, joy from sorrow

light from darkness
sunshine from rain
spring from winter
wellness from pain

life from brokenness
joy from the cross
sight from blindness
glory from loss

Christ Jesus rising
cross bearing fruit
Easter flowering
from bloodroot

LITURGY

All the way to Elizabeth
and in the months afterwards
she wove him, pondering,
"This is my body, my blood!"

Beneath the watching eyes
of donkey, ox, and sheep,
she rocked him, crooning,
"This is my body, my blood!"

In the moonless desert flight
and the Egypt days of his growing,
she nourished him, singing,
"This is my body, my blood!"

In the search for her young lost boy
and the foreboding day of his leaving,
she let him go, knowing,
"This is my body, my blood!"

Under the blood-smeared cross,
she rocked his mangled bones,
re-membering him, moaning,
"This is my body, my blood!"

When darkness, stones, and tomb
bloomed to Easter morning,
she ran to him, shouting,
"This is my body, my blood!"

Easter Song

The wilderness and the dry land shall be glad,
the desert shall rejoice and blossom. (ISAIAH 35:1)

Come to the garden with me!

Where we buried his humanity,
tombs have opened,
birds are singing.
Come and see!

Where we planted his humanity,
buds have opened,
flowers are blooming.
Come with me!

Come to the garden and see!

RESURRECTION

Death, that
old snake
skin, lies
discarded at
the garden-gate.

EASTER WITNESSES
(MARK 16 & MATTHEW 28)

The heady fragrances they carried
rose above their heads like incense,
exorcising the garden of death.
"Who will roll away the stone for us?"
the women whispered to one another.

Earlier, in the near-dawn darkness,
they had posed the question to the others—
as request, not challenge.
They had no heart to challenge the flock
hiding in terror behind secret doors.

None of the men had offered to go,
so the women had set out in haste alone
to straighten twisted feet and fingers,
comb black blood from matted hair,
anoint the precious body with spices.

"But who *will* roll away the stone?"
they whispered again as they neared the tomb.
"Jesus said prayer could move mountains.
We must stay together, continue to believe."
They stepped firmly forward, balancing their heavy jars.

When they looked up, they saw that the stone,
which was very large, had already been rolled back.
Inside, they heard from a being dressed in light:
"You are looking for Jesus who was crucified.
He has been raised; he is not here."
Fleeing from the tomb,
intent on telling no one,
they tripped pell-mell over terror and amazement
onto the glowing feet of Jesus.
"Go, tell the others!" he commanded.

After the telling, they set out in haste—
together this time, a community of equals—
to roll away stones, straighten crooked paths,
comb the far countries,
anoint the precious world with Good News.

The Women of Mark 16:8

"He is risen! He is not here!"
we heard—and fled
from the empty tomb,
our lips sealed by fear,
to cower in the upper room.

The Good News stayed dead
until, fed by the power
of Bread
broken,
we arose from our dread

and the Good News was spoken.

Emmaus Journey

(Luke 24:13–35)

All was chaos when he died.
We fled our separate ways at first,
then gathered again in the upper room
to chatter blue-lipped prayers
around the table where he'd talked
of love and oneness.

On the third day Cleopas and I
left for the home we'd abandoned
in order to follow him.
We wanted no part of the babble
the women had brought from the tomb.
We vowed to get on with our grieving.

On the road we met a Stranger
whose voice grew vaguely familiar
as he spoke of signs and suffering.
By the time we reached our village,
every tree and bush was blazing
and we pressed him to stay the night.

Yet not till we sat at the table
and watched the bread being broken
did we see the Light.

PRIMACY

(JOHN 20:3-8)

Though the other disciple won the race,
he waited at the tomb for Peter—
thus putting back in place the Rock
who, by his tumble out of grace,
had made himself a stumbling block.

Healing Touch
(John 20:24–28)

When Thomas touched
the wound in Jesus' side,
he learned what a lance
could do,

learned too
that the hole torn wide
had become the setting
for love's crown jewel.

THE ACCUSED

(MATTHEW 27:11–24)

(inspired by a pencil drawing by Randy Dixon)

I feared a riot when I heard the tumult.
The whole Sanhedrin came, shoving
the accused before me. My wife sent word:
"Have nothing to do with this innocent man.
I dreamed of him. . . ." She was free to dream.
It fell to me to preserve the Pax Romano.

The crowd accused him of sedition
and screamed at me to crucify him.
I tried to restore order, questioning
him: "Are you the King of the Jews?"
"You say so," he said, his eyes unafraid.
It was I who felt fear then.

I called for a bowl of water, dipped
my hands into it, held them up, dripping,
and proclaimed: "I am innocent
of this man's blood. Look to it yourselves."
When the water cleared, it was his face,
not mine, that looked up at me!

These many years since that fateful day,
I've called on all my stone-eared gods,
shouted my innocence to every water bowl.
But I am lost. After each ablution,
his face appears where mine should be.
"This," it says, "is what innocence looks like."

PONTIUS PILATE AT THE THERAPIST

You say it could as easily have been
Barabbas' blood the rabble asked for—
that it was their leaders who incited them.
But don't you see? That's it exactly, Sir!
The crowd called loud and clear for crucifixion.
One has to pay attention to a people
who obey like that. You did precisely
what you had to do. Now win their leaders'
loyalty and you've won the peace.
Sometimes a man, innocent or not,
has to die to pay the price of it.

The man *was* innocent, you say?
But don't forget you washed your hands of him—
a little water cleared you of the deed.
What a stroke of genius! Too bad
about your wife, though, washing her hands
a hundred times a day. No doubt in time
to come someone will make a play of it.
Tell her what's done is done—
what's one life less as long as it's not hers.
Perhaps you'd like to bring her too next time.

That's fifty denarii, please. Thank you, Sir.

Toward Reconciliation
(John 21:7)

He had watched Jesus heal his mother-in-law,
satisfy thousands with a few loaves and fish.
But no, he did not know him.

He had watched Jesus calm a storm at sea,
exorcise a wild man tormented by demons.
But no, he did not know him.

He had watched Jesus bring back a widow's son,
a twelve-year-old girl, their friend Lazarus.
But no, he did not know him.

With each denial he threw a year of his life on the fire.
Afterwards, he did not know himself.
If he had found a rope then . . . .

But Andrew had found him first.
And now this stranger standing on the shore—
who was he? Should he know him?

This man with authority in his voice,
telling them where to cast their nets—
who was he? Should he know him?

"It is the Lord!" he heard the beloved disciple say.
Lake water rinsed the ashes of his soul
as he swam toward One who knew him.

Rock Restored
(John 21:4–19)

Simon had only a moment
before the others came,
but when he stumbled onto the shore
to acknowledge his blame,
he forgot his practiced prose
and stood there in shattered shame.
The Sea of Tiberias dripping from his clothes,
he hung his head, wrung his hands
and, with twisting toes,
stuttered his sin in the sands.

Jesus chose not to mock
that sorry rubble of a man.
(*Here stands my invincible Rock*
who swore that, though others ran,
he would never desert me.) Instead,
he turned to the rest of the flock
and, knowing how they too must feel,
took some of the fish they had caught
(the coals were already red hot)
and served them a memorial meal.

When the whole sheepish lot had been fed,
Jesus took that disciple aside.
"Simon, son of John, do you love me?" he probed,
and when Simon too glibly replied,
asked the question over and over
till the chastened disciple cried,

"Lord, you know all things. You know I love you!"
"Then feed my sheep," Jesus said.

Thereafter Peter—the Rock restored—
gave God's love to a hungry world.

PENTECOST: HARVEST FESTIVAL
(ACTS 2:1–13)

Suddenly a rushing, rushing
shook the house where we were sitting
all together, waiting, praying
for the coming of the Spirit.

Wind and Fire leaped around us,
set our hearts ablaze and fearless,
danced us down into the streets
where Jews of every nation, tongue
had journeyed to Jerusalem
to celebrate the harvest feast.

Like autumn leaves blown by wind,
these children of the Exodus
swept around us, asked, amazed:
"What can this mean?" as we, consumed,
yet not consumed by blazing Fire,
burned the ancient Babel tower,
harvested God's holy people,
brought the flaming Word to all the world.

VII
MULLING THE WORD

THE HOMEMAKER GOD

(LUKE 15:8–10)

The Homemaker God has come to my house
to search for the lost coin of me
which I, in my miserly morning,
thinking this frugal and wise
and worthy of praise and grace,
hid in a safe "good place."

The Homemaker God has taken her broom
and swept from attic to basement,
moved cupboards and dressers,
stripped beds, emptied drawers—
now she's checking each pantry shelf
for the silver coin of myself.

The Homemaker God will find me, I trust—
she knows how to raise dust.

A WOMAN'S JOURNEY
IN DISCIPLESHIP

Jesus stood waiting for the woman's answer—
not looking past her, not laughing at her.
"Tell me what you need," he repeated, kindly,
"Come, what is it?"

"I don't need anything," she finally answered.
"I'm nothing but a . . ."
She didn't know how to finish the sentence.
She hung her head. "I'm nothing."

"Ah, you need a name," he said.
"I'll give you one: You-Are-Mine."
She thought he meant she was his slave,
so she followed the crowd that was following him.

After three days the people were hungry.
Jesus sat them down in small garden plots
and served fish and bread.
The woman ate with the rest.

When Jesus found her, he asked again,
"Do you know now what you need?"

"Please, Sir, I'm still hungry,"
she answered shyly.

He held out more bread.
"Take! Eat!" he told her.

"Let him put it down," she thought.
"I'm unclean."

It lay in his hands.
"Take it," Jesus urged.

She broke off a piece—
careful not to touch him—
and chewed it slowly, letting the mash
fill her mouth with its goodness.
He watched her swallow it
and asked, "Still hungry?"
She nodded.
"Take more."

When she reached for the bread,
her fingers touched his!
She backed away, frightened,
and awkwardly stumbled.

His right arm encircled her,
hemming her in.
"You-Are-Mine," he said,
"tell me what you need."

"If you please, Sir," she said,
"give me bread like this always."

"Those who follow me
never go hungry,"
he answered her, smiling.
"I am Living Bread."

HOLY GROUND
(Exodus 3:1–5)

I went to the desert one morning
and walked with Moses in the sand
to where the bush was burning.
That it did not turn to ash
was no surprise to me
for so I'd seen it burning
throughout my childhood days.

But suddenly a voice called out to me
from that bush!
Moses left.
Take off your shoes, I heard,
for the life on which you stand is holy.
I am the ONE WHO IS
and this is how I hold you.

I stood barefoot on the ground
of my life history,
burning through and through
with that mystery.

LEARNING TO TRUST

(LUKE 5:12–13)

All my leprosies cry out,
"You can heal me if you want to."

"Want to?" you say.
"Of course I do. Be healed."

So simple!
Nothing much required of me—

show my oozing needs to you,
trust that you will make me whole.

Yahweh, My Heritage, My Cup
(Psalm 16)

After the first snow of this decembered
time, the textured grass is spread
like Irish linen on the field You
set before me. I feast on trees
moving in wind and wander down
to drink the wine stored in
dark root cellars.
Your Spirit
warms
my
blood
O
God!
O God!

APPLE PICKING: EDEN REVISITED

All day we played in paradise—
climbed up ladders into skies
of apple tree; shook, threw,
caught, ate the tempting fruit;
and laughed to see the legendary
serpent shrunk to harmless worms.

At evening, riding wagons home
with baskets crowned to overflowing,
we let go (without our knowing)
of the myth of up-and-downness—
saw God's graces in the roundness
of apples, baskets, earth, embraces.

In This Fog
(Luke 12:22–32)

In this fog I barely see
ten feet in front of me.
But it doesn't really matter
where I go, how far-—
whether I walk
to the end of the block
or the nearest star.

In this fog it doesn't matter
how fast I go or where.
There's no hurry.
Not to worry!
God sees what's ahead of me
and will get me there.

EMMANUEL: GOD WITH US
(GALATIANS 3:26–28)

In Bethlehem
a baby's cry
shatters barriers.

Women, men
of every creed,
culture, race

gaze across
the rubbled walls
in wonder,

finding every face
luminous
with godliness!

A DIFFERENT KIND OF KING

(for the Feast of Christ the King)

On a night filled with stars,
Christ broke through our defenses,
disarming us with infant cries.
Kings from foreign countries
came to give him homage
but left again without a trace.

Years went by. Fearing nothing,
we regrouped, returned to battles.
He reappeared in the countryside,
recruiting the peasants
and sabotaging our strategies
by commands to love the enemy.

We infiltrated his company,
set him up as "King of the Jews"
and nailed him for it on execution hill.
Now, rumors whisper,
he has eastered back behind our lines
to plot a reign of peace.

FEAST OF ST. PAUL

This morning I had planned to pray
with Paul, knocked off his horse.

But oh! the birds, scarcely knowing what to do
with wings grown used to flying in a sodden sky
through days and days of rain on rain on rain,
circled, swooped, alit on bush and weed,
and filled the sun-rinsed air with fireworks
of melody that burst and bloomed and twinkled out
in slow descent into my prayer.

I tumbled into grace a different way
(whether in or out of the body, I don't know)
and saved Paul's route for a rainy day.

On the Way to Easter

Bible in hand,
I slip behind a wall of time
to walk with the women.

"Are you afraid?" I ask,
panting to keep up with them—
strong from three years of walking.

"Of course," they answer,
"but his body must be anointed!"
They keep walking.

"There's no one to roll away
the stone," I object.
(Are they courageous or just naive?)

"There's no one else to anoint him,"
they counter firmly
and keep walking.

Ahead I see sunlight
glinting off steel. "There's no one
to protect you!" I protest.

They nod and keep walking,
their burdens perfectly balanced.
(Courageous, I decide.)

"Godspeed then," I say
as I shift my life on my shoulders
and retreat to my safe, familiar world.

But the road on which I find myself
is crowded with people in need
of every kind of anointing.

"Godspeed!" I hear the women call
across the millennial wall
as I start walking.

GOD OF SHELTER, GOD OF SHADE
(ISAIAH 4:6)

God of shelter from the rain,
God of shade from the heat,

I run from You
through the muddy street
of my uncommitted heart
till wild winds beat
against my doors,
blasting sand
through all my walls,
and I stand
without retreat,
hear Your command
to be the wheat.

Sweet the giving!
Sweet this land!

God of shelter from the rain.
God of shade from the heat.

COMPANION
(LUKE 4:2–4)

I thought this hunger mine alone
until I saw your desert table spread
with loaves of stones you could have changed to bread.

LIFE-GIVING

I must be eaten to give nourishment.

Sometimes I'm bitten bitterly,
swallowed in large chunks,
regurgitated.

Sometimes I'm eaten casually,
tossed in with other junk food,
quickly forgotten.

Sometimes I'm chewed reverently
by one who hungers
for what I want to share.

That's communion!

Someday the race will be
one Bread, one Body,
and in the eating there will be no pain.

A Celibate Dialogues with God

I asked God:
    "Must I be my last and only word?
    Will this who-I-am be heard
    no more when I am dead?
    Who will know what I have said?
    Who will weave my melody into their song
    or hum at least my harmonies along
    with theirs? Who will? Who will?"

And God said: "Peace. Be still."

Paschal Mystery

I am
growing,
eating the
white and yolk
inside this earth-
house; the shell is
beginning to harden a
bit, cramping me just
enough to let me know
this home is not for-
ever—someday I must
crack it open to
enter a larger
world.

PRAYER FOR A HAPPY DEATH
(JOHN 20:6–7)

When I arrive at the tomb,
petered out of breath like Peter,
let me enter it in awe,
see the worn garments of myself
neatly folded, laid aside,
and follow you anew in Galilee.

WAIT FOR ME, JESUS

Wait for me, Jesus,
on your way to the tree.
Don't move out of sight.

Up, I know,
is the only way to grow,
but I'm so loaded down with me

and it is night.

As It Was in the Beginning

I spiral back
      toward the black
                        mire
            from which You drew me,
                                    threw me
                  on Your potter's wheel;
                        feel
                  Your hot
      nearness now,
Your fire;
            know not
                        the how
                        of death,
                  know only that I must
            return this dust,
return to Breath.

As Jesus Dies

He hangs high
between earth and sky,
waiting to die.

Some play games.
Some call him names.
Some stand by.

Where am I?

"Unless the Grain of Wheat Falls"

Easter!
But I'm still torn with grief,
disbelief.
I'm not ready yet!
I clutch the old familiar pain—
I've gotten used to the dark,
grown calluses against the rub of walls.
I feel secure confined within the grain.

Easter!
This unseen Presence signed in Bread,
this utter homey-ness of meal
still leaves a loneliness that gnaws.
It almost would be easier
had you stayed dead.
I would not have to try to learn
to know you in this strange new way

and when my time came, I could say
good-bye behind a finished smile,
without a thought or care
for those I had not fed.
But now to have to live from day to day
on Bread and promise of Bread—
to eat and pass the loaves along
and not to store!

This call to grow to Easter ripeness
shakes my familiar ground,
quakes the very kernel of myself.
I thought I had secured my walls so well.
But you roll away, like a child's toy,
the rock I had sealed against you
and make me an empty shell of wheat
to witness that you are alive in me.

In His Mother's Arms

Mary, Earth Mother,
take your Son's dead weight
together with ours
to your heart.

Take our sins and stupidities,
stillbirths and betrayals,
diseases and dementias,
tumors and terrors,
hunger and hopelessness
to your heart.

Hold us together—
Redeemer and redeemed—
in your heart,
Mary, Earth Mother.

OUR FATHER OUR MOTHER

Our Father Our Mother,
so wholly in heaven,
so on-the-way,
so be-coming
in every him-her-you-me
that ever on earth
was, is, will-be,

knead us every this-day
into one bread.

Commissioning

This bread and wine is sign
of my new covenant with you:
I am with you always!
Tell the people whom I send into your life
that this is so.

I loved the world so much I chose
to enter humanness.
I walked the earth, worked, prayed,
loved, laughed, cried.
Word made Flesh, I handed over
day and night to God for you.
Tell the people whom I send into your life
that this is so.

On the night before I died
I took my life into my hands.
Eat my body! Drink my blood!
I said, and gave it all for you.
For you I was handed over,
crushed, poured out, broken.
Tell the people whom I send into your life
that this is so.

I have given all!
Tell everyone whom I will give to you
that this is so.
Do—in memory of me—
what I have done. Go!

EPILOGUE

"I Am with You Always, to the End of the Age"

I Am with You Always
(Matthew 28:20)

I am with you when you're running out of wine
at your child's wedding feast
and you know the shame of it will last forever.
I will be for you the Best Wine of all.

I am with you in your storm-tossed boat
when joy, hope, life seem lost at sea
and you come close to falling overboard.
I will still the storm, restore you to tranquility.

I am with you when you're caught out on a limb—
a social climbing tax collector, treed!
I too will climb a tree and be mocked on it.
I will honor you by coming to your house to eat.

I am with you when your body is so bent
that friendly faces, trees, sky are lost to view
and all you see are feet hurrying by.
I will empower you to stand up straight again.

I am with you when men catch you in adultery
and your death is but a stone's throw away.
I am the Gate to the sheepfold. I will lay
my body down between your enemies and you.

I am with you when you claim you do not know me.
I have prayed that you may overcome despair
and bring the heavy burden of your sin to me.
I have forgiven you ahead of time.

I am with you when your dearest friend and brother
passes through the dark door of death,
leaving you disconsolate. I know the pain of loss.
I AM the Resurrection and the Life.